OUT OF PARADISE

41 poems of
distress, humor, and hope

MICHAEL COSTANZO

FootHills Publishing

Acknowledgments

I would like to acknowledge the many people who have supported me during the months of my illness with their prayer, their get-well cards, or gifts of fruit and flowers.

In particular I like to thank the Sisters of Mercy of the Americas at Blossom Road, Rochester, N.Y. for their warm welcome to their McAuley Residence, their encouragement, and their spiritual support.

To all, my heartfelt Thank You.

© Copyright 2008 Michael Costanzo

Cover photo – by Michael Czarnecki
"Water Ouzel along Gallatin River"

ISBN: 0-941053-60-1

FootHills Publishing
P. O. Box 68
Kanona, NY 14856
www.foothillspublishing.com

*To my sister Josephine
And her husband Gino
With grateful thanks
For the love and compassion
Shown me
During my illness*

Contents

Foreword   6

Part I: A Journey Through Darkness

I Not Yet	11
II Thump	12
III Josephine	13
IV CTICU Crew	14
V Sand and Air	15
VI Visits	16
VII Space Mask	17
VIII First Steps	18
IX Is This Food?	19
X Death Toll	20
XI Up and Away	21
XII Privacy	22
XIII A Hymn of Praise	23
XIV Nights in White	24
XV Floor Techs	25
XVI New Blood	26
XVII Four in White	27
XVIII Men in Black	28
XIX Doctors	29
XX CABG	30

Part II: Towards the Light

XXI A New Journey	33
XXII Sisters in Plenty	34
XXIII A Time for REST	35
XXIV Blessings	36
XXV Prayer	37
XXVI Daily Mass	38
XXVII Friend	39
XXVIII Cheerful Robin	40
XXIX Shamrock	41
XXX Babysitter	42
XXXI Dissolution	43
XXXII Anointing	44
XXXIII Mater Dolorosa	45
XXXIV Distances	46
XXXV (A Paren[t]-	47
XXXVI -Thesis)	48
XXXVII Handsome Trio	49
XXXVIII Lunch at 950	50
XXXIX Philip	51
XL Jo & Gino	52
XLI Surrender	53
Author's Bio	55

Foreword

> "Castigans castigavit me Dominus,
> et morti non tradidit me."
> (Psalm 118,18)

It is a known fact that pain and suffering are constitutive elements of our human existence. The modes, intensity, and quality may vary from person to person, and affect individuals and families in more or less profound ways.

Pain shapes our physical reality in ways that affect our daily living by diminishing our dedication to work, our enjoyment of life, our very desire to exist. Suffering defines who we are, how we envision the present and the future world, what we believe and hope. It can make us strong or break us down. It's the very essence of life; either we sing, or we sink under.

For more than seven months during the unfolding of this year 2007 I have encountered both pain and suffering, like many other individuals in this world of ours. A trial no more nor less poignant than others have faced or endured. While both pain and suffering have paled in comparison to many tragic events that have befallen huge numbers of people all over the world, I have equally felt them in my body, soul, and spirit; and seen my life turned upside down and drastically changed.

These poems, written between March 25th and May 22nd 2007, are personal and intimate expressions of the transformation that has taken place in me, and still does. I offer them to anyone who wishes to read them – as if looking in a mirror and seeing one's own image both reflected and refracted.

October 2007
M.C.

The human frailty we experience during times of illness can strip us of our masks and bring us to the core of our authenticity if we are able to embrace our vulnerability and befriend it. In sharing his story, Rev. Costanzo, through his recent suffering, gives us a glimpse of how he was able to touch into the healing presence of Christ from the darkness of his physical plight. His heightened awareness of God's compassionate care for him in the people and situations he encountered along the way are testimonies to us of the all embracing love God has for us even when we may not feel it. His reflections will be a source of strength and hope for all those who contemplate his words.

                              Mary Fran Wegman, RSM, RN

Part I: A Journey Through Darkness

I Not Yet

May I please come in?
>Said I with a broken voice.
>A clear sound came through
>The transparent white cloud.
>Why? Who are you?
Surprised, I answered My time has come
>And my name should be with you.
>I hear the sounds of celebration
>A mighty choir shaking the foundations
>Of the blue planet below.
I have read all the names on the list
>But found your name not.
>You must be mistaken – Look below
>And see someone by your bed waiting
>In prayer and tears for your return.
Go back to your watery planet,
>For you must continue your journey
>'Til the path you thread on is worn out
>And your heart is filled with longing.
>Go on, let yourself gently through the air.

II Thump

Easier said than done. The descent begun
    My dilated pupils absorbed the colors around,
    Intense green and yellow gold
    Delicate blue and shades of it.
    It was a breathtaking sight.
Then a whirlwind caught me tight
    And long before I realized it
    We passed through the ozone layer depleted.
    Its speed ever high and its might
    Scorched me as it threw me flat on my...

III Josephine

She said I'd been asleep for the length of a week
    Longing to hear those words of creation,
    And saw that what God had made was good.
She waited day after day for my return
    Pained by my total silence and lack of light
    As mother did when I was fifteen.
Treasure your grandchild, sister, even for me
    May the joy of his young days be yours
    And lighten the burden I have placed on you.

IV CTICU Crew

Back from the trip I saw fluttering wings,
    Vivid green and yellows flooded my closed eyes,
    And turned to usual white and gray with the light of day.
Bill was there, a PA warm with compassion;
    Said Hi, Father, and I didn't know why. Who was I?
    A samurai by his Japanese mother
    He has uncommon strength in calmness,
    By his Irish father a strong faith in Christ.
    I liked the Celtic cross he wore and his real concern.
Rebecca, Virginia and Linda who cared for me
    When like a child I was totally dependent. What
    Grace and care they showed, what love for a
    Pained human body, a skeleton of existence.
Welcome back, father, welcome back! Why?
    Was I here before? Where did I go?

V Sand and Air

All things stored away, I lay on my bed
    And enjoyed the steady lulling of the cruise ship
    The sea water beating the flanks of the vessel
    Created a rhythm that put all gods to sleep…
Perhaps I had dreams, perhaps my spirit found peace.
    Someone must have knocked at the door –
    No sea, no cruise ship, only a sudden start.
    On my special bed, warm air heated sand,
    Perhaps soothing the pain of bedsores.

VI Visits

Visitors came and shook their heads –
    What were those blankets covering?
    They came and went as people do at wakes
    Wishing Josephine the best for me.

Priests poured in to pray and anoint – so much
    Kindness in their heart. Bob and Richard,
    Twins in nature twins in faith, each came twice –
    Or was I drunk with wine and saw double?

Ross who knelt by my bedside and talked with me
    And prayed – our thoughts to Jessie who's with God.
    Good friend, who humbled me with his affection,
    But my heart is richer because of his love.

VII Space Mask

Seven days for creation and rest – God took time
    Order embraced the universe and Beauty shone
    From a leaf of grass to the mighty centennial tree.
Lord, they said, it has been in the tomb for four days
    And by now it must be corrupted to the core.
    Remove the bandage of those linen strips, and let him go.
Seven days wrapped in electronic strips I lay in space –
    Masks and feeding tubes, oxygen and contraptions,
    New Lazarus I come to life from a world of death.

VIII First Steps

Born again at sixty three I need my walker's
    Support and an escort to put the left ahead
    And like a sheep let the right move along.
    Blessedness of moving around and greeting others.
With me a nurse and IV pole, a heart monitor
    And a bag of liquids that must be disposed.
    Here is Virginia dressed in white checking my steps,
    And I hanging on to the cart with my life signs.
A short one hundred seems a mile to these weak legs
    My heart says yes and my feet comply – one,
    Two, three steps and more – almost a marathon.

IX Is This Food?

It must be – so say the labels and the menu.
    Ah, the fragrance of plastic and cardboard taste!
    Is there anything that I can actually eat?
Anesthesia and invading tubes and all sorts of pills
    Keep coming in my direction, multi shower
    Particles of an exploded comet in the sky.
But eat one must – you know, your body needs protein
    From the mystery food stuff properly arranged
    Under a plastic dome and exhaling vapors from Hades.

X Death Toll

Day follows day, blood samples by the dozens,
    Glucose tests, temp, and the repeated vital signs
    By alternating nurses, PAs and floor techs.
But the night is endless – every wink takes two minutes
    Although the clock still reads two past two.
    I read but the eyes get cloudy, I close them but cannot sleep.
What is this sound steady and monotonous imprinted
    In my brain? Is it the bell that announces death?
    Someone stop it, it's filling to the brim my memory cells.

XI Up and Away

They say it's Monday, March 12 – time to leave the ICU.
    It's not easy to leave the cocoon – I'm neither
    Larva nor caterpillar, not the soaring butterfly in the blue.
I shall come and see you on the fourth floor, says Bill
    And his words are echoed by Rebecca's smile and Virginia.
    I'll look forward to their visits, and come they shall.
Energetic Nancy in organized strokes gets the caravan ready,
    Accomplishes the task while a seagull beats its wings
    And lifts itself majestically in the air – I in my new room.

XII Privacy

Your name and your date of birth, said Mollie
   All dressed in white, round glasses and a cheerful face.
   My name is MC and was born a few light years ago in 43.
The information is loose of chain, sips through the medicinal air,
   Reaches close and distant ears, everyone knows a fact or two.
   In my small room I lie on my bed unable to react.
Then comes the shower ceremony – I can barely stand.
   I sit on a stool and let the grace of God's water refresh me –
   Nobody said that there one could preserve a bit of modesty.

XIII A Hymn of Praise

Gone are the splendid colors imprinted in my memory.
    Now majestic sounds in harmony divine submerge me
    Breakers of an ocean of voices lashing with force.
Certainly it is the blessed gathered before the Lamb
    Thousands before the throne singing God's praises
    For salvation received and joy now together shared.
Ah! Me miserable being! I only hear repeated
    A thousand times a day the first two bars of the song
    In an endless reminder of joys not yet enjoyed.

XIV Nights in White

In this unusual vacation, time has no place
    Days for restful sleep and nights in white
    A stream of visitors from doctors to nurses and friends.
But the night is long and dawn never comes – never.
    I read the story of Rodion, Dunia, and Sonia
    By paragraphs and chapters, and share their pain.
My eyelids close at 2:02 and I fall asleep
    No dreams restore my peace and bring me rest.
    A gentle stroke on my hand at 2:10 needs my blood.

XV Floor Techs

Kim was on the floor on my first day in 4400,
> Young and eager for the work she does, the dream ahead,
> Helped quietly for a number of needs, lifting my spirit.

Nereida shaved me twice without a knick, made me human
> Again (I was a cave man), wrote Dios te bendiga.
> Kesha came always at night claiming vials of blood

For the daily supply of tests, and tests, and tests.
> Gentle Alicia, half Italian and a quarter French,
> Never made the needle sting – The other quarter?!

And then appeared Eulice who could not leave the floor
> Without praying over me – I felt joy within.
> There is magic in a name; soothing sound in hers.

XVI New Blood

It flows silent through my arteries and my veins.
> This patched-up heart pumps refreshed and clean
> The new red liquid that keeps my broken body alive.

Is any of my own blood left in me? Someone
> Who cared for a human life provided the stock
> That abundantly was transfused in me, a relic of self.

New blood, a repaired heart in need of much help,
> Appearance of normality in the 'good color' of my face –
> Is this what life should really be? Am I truly alive?

XVII Four in White

As I lie helpless in bed on this sand-air mattress
    The steady monotonous sound sails me on a cruise–
    Ship of happier days from one Caribbean island to the next.
My eyes close momentarily and I see white uniforms…
    Time for your medication, says my first lady in white,
    Beth whose smile helps the bitter pills go down.
And Mollie secure in her work checks my blood pressure,
    Andrea hides a heart full of compassion behind a mask
    Of indifference, but Ann soothes the late hours of day –
        The calm and serenity of her spirit glows
        On the smooth features of her face.

XVIII Men in Black

'I slept' for a week. Josephine by my bedside
    In anguish for decisions to take and sorrows to feel.
    Angels came by flapping their wings and fanning hope.
Robert and Richard true to their common nature
    Came twice bringing comfort and God's strength,
    Anointing me and feeding me the Body of Christ.
Fred all the way from the lakeside with another blessing,
    Cheerful Bill from closer by brought news and laughter,
    And a younger Fred laden with prayers from a whole parish.

XIX Doctors

They come and go by the cubicles of our illness
    Faster than lightning on a gorgeous summer day
    With a trail of residents and Pas for a quick peek.
At a glance they tell if good health is anywhere near
    Reassuring the hopeful, mesmerizing the weak,
    And as gods of yore proceed on to more work to do.
Dr. David knows my heart better than I do,
    He anguished by my bedside till it beat again
    Stroking my hair as a father his feverish child's.

XX CABG

Coronary Artery Bypass Graft was the acronym around
    And my untrained Sicilian ear heard it 'cabbage.'
    Marvel, man, no longer a heart but a cabbage in my chest!
Tricks of the mind conjure up moments of the un-known –
    Will this vegetable heart feel human emotions again?
    What love will it be capable to give and receive?
'Tis but a perfect pump that works without rest
    And sends the vital lymph to limbs near and far –
    Ah! This mended heart has much work to do till the final beat.

Part II: Towards the Light

XXI A New Journey

The time has come, tomorrow you will go home.
    The sound is sweet, the prospect warmer yet –
    To see again familiar pictures, hear real sounds.
But home is a mirage and a future dream.
    Pressure sores a heartless gift of careless care
    Humble me day after day and keep me down to earth.
A new journey begins as I travel from a hospital
    To a rehab place – no home, no possessions,
    No visible horizon crowd my mind nor stir my feelings.

XXII Sisters in Plenty

Here is the place I'll be calling home for a time to come
    Where simplicity and space interweave with plenty –
    There is no room for sadness or despair, for God is near.
These are sisters whose life of work was offered to the Lord
    Whose bodies weakened, broken, and often pained
    Carry the marks of Christ's wounds with hidden joy.
Here is Mary Jude who often sits before the Lord's presence
    In silent dialogue with the Healer and Lover divine,
    There is the crowd of Annes, Conceptas, and Dominicas,
        Praising the Source of Life and Love.

XXIII A Time for REST

My days have not been mine since February twenty seven –
    Dr. Gene with great care drove me to a place of care –
    Others have dictated my coming and going, my breathing.
Five long weeks have passed me by – I resting idle in bed.
    But time has come to rise to the task, mind over matter,
    And let each day become the focus of work and hope.
I sit at the computer and let my fingers nimbly be guided
    By a mind still alert and willing to create –
    In a couple of weeks my college campus will read 'Verbum.'

XXIV Blessings

Blessings come in bunches like grapes – I've no idea
    If anyone ever said that; is it even true?
    But mine have, during this time of forced rest.
They have come in groups or alone, family and friends,
    Colleagues from work, from churches and homes,
    Each with a gift of comfort, a card, or a word of hope.
Tony and Bruna came one day with a load of goods and care,
    Picked me up to dine and watch soccer games
    Renewed my faith that tomorrow will come once again.

XXV Prayer

In this universe I now inhabit, Time has no bearing –
  Good wishes, inquiries, advice follow through the day –
  Then comes night with her veil of darkness; silence reigns.
Spirit awakes and probes the mystery of life and death,
  The mind offers no help but in stillness mutes the quest.
  Turn to prayer, whispers soul, deliver yourself into His hands.
Early night is often too long, I find no rest in this bed.
  No clock tics the minutes away, sleep only a mirage.
  I take in hand my rosary beads, begin Aves, drift asleep.

XXVI Daily Mass

Intellectually stimulating his words open new ways
    Through the spacious skies of faith, enrich my soul
    When this falcon plummets from heights and probes depths.
Every word is a song, a perfect sonnet to my poet ears
    As I stand in stillness of being before the altar of love
    Waiting like a newborn chick to be fed with manna of life.
Strings are laid across the worlds of my existence
    The divine player comes with solicitude eager to perform
    A song of grace, a hymn of thanks resounding in harmony.

XXVII Friend

I no longer keep record, like a child who can only
    Count to ten and make his parents proud,
    For his presence by my world has been my plenty.
Wise was the ancient sage who counted richest treasure
    A friend as true and trusted as this prince has been,
    Filling the void of knowledge of this weakened body.
His words couched in simple unadorned attire
    Probe the depth of spirit, give wings to the mind –
    His blessing brief, hardly hides his caring concern.

Fr. Bill,
May the Lord bless you in many wonderful ways.
Christmas 2007
Michael

XXVIII Cheerful Robin

Light on her feet, with a smile that soothes pain
    She comes to all in need of care through the day
    Her nursing skills reassuring our battered bodies.
I wonder how she stretches the hours of day and night
    To be with everyone time and again, from branch to tree
    Like a winged creature in the vast blue space.
Her God the strength that moves each moment of her day,
    Gratitude for a new lease on life the source of hope,
    Clothed with a zest for life and the joy of loving freely.

XXIX Shamrock

He takes brief flights from this round wooden stick
    To the one above and then the metal bars of his cage,
    This trapped canary, and sings to the sound of music.
She takes good care of you, the petite a bit curved by age
    Sister DePaul – like a parent she feeds you delicious food,
    Even prays with you as you sing your happy songs for us.
I often wonder if you miss the spacious open skies
    And the fragrance of budding trees and new green leaves,
    The busy flights of plumed companions, the joy of freedom.

XXX Babysitter

Everywhere I go these days I carry with me
    My docile, folded, lightweight sitter
    Ready to step in when the faucet begins to drip.
Where is Lady Dignity hiding these gloomy days?
    I am in want of her treasured presence and company,
    My home is empty, steeped in silence and negligence.
Father who nourish our short human existence,
    Did your heart sink in sorrow and pain
    When they stripped Your Son and fixed him on wooden bars?

XXXI Dissolution

Loss of weight, a nasty nausea, and lack of appetite,
    A trident twisted in my dissolving body
    By an invisible hand at work against me.
Gentle Father, you teach me patience and renew my faith.
    How long will you let your hand cause this havoc?
    Will you not spare me a moment of relief and breath?
I am your son, though prodigal many a time,
    And long to see the calmness of your face
    And feel the warmth of your forgiving hug.

XXXII Anointing

Sisters, lay people, and priests assembled here
> Hang on to fragments of life by threads of hope
> Waiting for bodies to mend and spirits to heal.

Is there anyone among you who is sick and ailing?
> Let the elders gather around him imposing
> Their outstretched hand imploring God's blessing.

Lord of life, broken and given, how do you hold back
> Your tears of grief before the misery of the world?
> Forgive our wandering and heal our longing souls.

XXXIII Mater Dolorosa

In the blink of an eye she was no longer of this world.
    No angels by her singing either threnody or paean,
    Only a youth transfixed to the core by the horrid unknown.
And yet, only a handful of days before she'd come to me
    With prayers and cheerful wishes for my recovery
    Like a breath of crisp spring air after a winter waste.
By your cross, Kristine, I see your sorrowful parents
    And no words are apt to console them for you are not –
    Like Kristos you bequeath to them your orphaned son
        As you enter before the Presence
        In fullness of life.

XXXIV Distances

Miles separate us and an ocean of silence,
    There is no script for the near future,
    We must act this dream each on our own.
I think of you, beloved sister, who walked this road
    A time ago – you shame anyone by your zest for life,
    Your daily work, and the courage in your soul.
My longing for you and your beloved family
    Rests imprisoned in my heart – some day I shall
    Sit again with my book of prayer by your fireplace.

XXXV (A Paren[t]-

If the good 'look' everyone notes and openly admires
    Were the real key to my full recovery and health,
       I would for sure be settled back in my home and garden.
There my memories of mom and dad – though hid from sight
    They live in me through every moment of my day,
       They fill the voids in my mind, give rest to my heart.
But a good 'look' is only apparent, a synthesis without a premise.
    'Tis the day of your birth, mother, and this illness
       I believe to be by your prayer only a parenthesis.

XXXVI -Thesis)

Reality hits me hard these days – dreams sag, uncertainty thrives.
    I have no illusions left in store and dread appearances of security.
    Time stands still in this parenthesis – no one knows why.
Supreme Parent who govern the world, and bring order to chaos,
    I lament my lack of faith before you and grieve for my sin,
    I raise my hands in supplication hiding my tears and my hope.
I search for meaning in my quest for the goodness of your will.
    This is my thesis and my comfort – Your love has saved me,
    Your plan and purpose trustworthy, your hand a sure guide.

XXXVII Handsome Trio

They finally came up from Philly, PA – a long trek –
    The little one only two months old, like a rising sun,
    She the pupil of my eye, and he my friend.
My longing for closeness becomes reality before my eyes,
    My arms hold a little bundle of love who smiles
    And pushes strong on his legs, gazes at objects 'round.
I see the two equally taken by this beautiful baby –
    Their care for a safe today, their dream for tomorrow
    Nurtured with love, they the strings of a lyre
        Singing a new song to life.

XXXVIII Lunch at 950

The table is set – silverware, plates and glasses
    All in place for our family meal at half past one –
    Fragrant aromas rise from the oven and tease our palate.
I am king of this reign for a long thirty minutes,
    Others are gone to see Crissy and Joe's new home,
    Gino and Jo with them, and Phil will soon arrive with Jenna.
We sit to enjoy God's grace and offer a prayer of thanks –
    A small family of six, and me the zio grown old –
    But the center of attention is he, the two-month old baby.

XXXIX Philip

I miss your presence this weekend, and your visit –
    I miss our chats on things irrelevant as the
    Amerks loss that ends their season early once again.
We will ponder on the Bills' selections this year
    As the NFL draft drags on to a second day, and
    Will, the two of us, remain skeptic on the Sabres' hopes…
Silently, we will speak of subjects that matter –
    Your hopes and dreams for the morrow, the approaching
    Preoccupations of a wedding day, the love you feel,
        And a life of joys and sorrows
        With your heart's beloved.

XL Jo & Gino

Daily, faithfully, my sister and husband by my bed
    Hoping for progress in my health state,
    Making plans for the day of my final release.
Emotions transpire even when tongues are still.

Josephine and Gino, my help and my hope
    Have taken the burden of worries from me
    Adding a load to theirs without a complaint.
For weeks a bed ready for me in their welcoming home.

What is it like to love as they do without limit?
    Can it be only a matter of blood? Perhaps this blood
    Thicker than death is real lymph of life.

Years come and go, and our brown hair turns to gray,
    Our aches multiply from day to day, yet life finds
    Fulfillment in your love today, our hope for days to come.

XLI Surrender

Beloved God who probe and read our hearts
    You have finally brought me to my knees.
    "Horrendum est incidere in manus Dei viventis."
    I know I have loved you in many precious ways
    And served your people's needs for love of you.
    Your grace flowed abundantly on whatever I did.

Still you were not content, as you knew I withheld
    Within my stubborn mind and recesses of my soul
    The one precious pearl, the only gift you wanted.
    It was always my treasure, my joy and pride,
    The one gift your gave me that I'd never give away,
    What made me real and informed my being.

Here is to you this gift, this pearl, this treasure.
    I have no choice in the matter, you're the stronger.
    I have not lost my battle, but raise the white flag.
    Take it, my God, and with it the burden it is.
    I place in your hands my life, my being,
    And cast at your feet my all, my independence.

Author's Bio

Michael Costanzo was born and educated in Sicily (Italy), where he taught from 1962-1970. At the end of 1970 he came to the USA to join his parents and family, already living in Rochester since 1962. After receiving a PhD in 1979 and a Doctorate in Biblical Theology in 1987 from the University of St. Thomas in Rome, he returned to Rochester and began teaching at St. John Fisher College, Nazareth College, MCC, and BOCES. He has been a full time teacher in the Department of Religious Studies at St. John Fisher College since the Fall semester of 2001. Rev. Costanzo is a Roman Catholic Priest of the Diocese of Piazza Armerina in Sicily (Italy), and has been serving in the Diocese of Rochester, NY since 1971.

One of his books of poetry, "A Vision of Beauty," was published by FootHills Publishing in 2006.